WELCOME TO THE WORLD

Penguins

Diane Swanson

WALRUS
BOOKS

Edited by Elizabeth McLean
Cover design by Steve Penner
Interior design by Margaret Ng
Typeset by Jacqui Thomas
Cover photograph by Wayne Lynch
Photo credits: Wayne Lynch iv, 10, 12, 20, 22, 26; Joe Sroka/Dembinsky Photo Assoc. 2; John Gerlach/Dembinsky Photo Assoc. 4; Hal Beral/aaaimagemakers.com 6; Peter Oxford/Nature Picture Library 8; Mark J. Thomas/Dembinsky Photo Assoc. 14; Lynn M. Stone 16, 18; Fritz Polking/Dembinsky Photo Assoc. 24.

Printed and bound in Canada

Library and Archives Canada Cataloguing in Publication

Swanson, Diane, 1944–
    Welcome to the world of penguins/Diane Swanson.

    Includes index.
    ISBN 1-55285-450-7
    ISBN 978-1-55285-450-1

    1. Penguins—Juvenile literature. I. Title.

QL696.S473S92 2003   j598.47   C2002-911408-X

The publisher acknowledges the financial support of the Canada Council for the Arts, the British Columbia Arts Council, and the Government of Canada through the Canada Book Fund (CBF). Whitecap Books also acknowledges the financial support of the Province of British Columbia through the Book Publishing Tax Credit.

 Canada Council for the Arts   Conseil des Arts du Canada    BRITISH COLUMBIA ARTS COUNCIL

ENVIRONMENTAL BENEFITS STATEMENT

Whitecap Books Ltd saved the following resources by printing the pages of this book on chlorine free paper made with 10% post-consumer waste.

WATER	SOLID WASTE	GREENHOUSE GASES
90	6	20
GALLONS	POUNDS	POUNDS

Environmental impact estimates were made using the Environmental Paper Network Paper Calculator. For more information visit www.papercalculator.org.

Contents

World of Difference

PENGUINS FLY THROUGH WATER, NOT AIR. Unlike most other birds, penguins have no flight feathers and no true wings. Instead, they have stiff, narrow flippers designed for fast swimming—flying—underwater.

On land and on ice, penguins waddle along on short legs and webbed feet. Sharp claws help them grip, but the birds may trip over rocks and knobs of ice.

Some penguins walk just a little; others walk a lot. Adélie (uh-DAY-lee) penguins might travel across 100 kilometres (60 miles) of ice to reach water, walking as fast as

Sw-o-o-sh! Adélie penguins toboggan on their fat bellies.

1

people do—about 5 kilometres (3 miles) per hour.

When penguins are in a hurry to cross a stretch of ice, they s-l-i-d-e on their tummies. They push off with their feet, often paddling and balancing with their flippers. Some kinds of penguins can toboggan faster than people can ski over level land.

Earth's smallest kind of penguin is well named—little penguin.

Of the world's 17 kinds of penguins, the biggest are the emperor penguins. They stand up to 120 centimetres (4 feet) tall. The smallest are called little, blue, or fairy penguins. They are only one-third as tall as emperor penguins.

Most penguins are black and white, but some, such as king penguins, sport flashes of yellow and orange feathers around their necks. Others, including royal and macaroni penguins, have yellow-orange plumes on the tops of their heads.

Penguins charm people. Here are some of the reasons why:

- Penguins grow their feathers in thick jumbles—not in neat rows—helping the birds keep extra dry and warm.
- Huddled together on antarctic ice sheets, emperor penguins can survive in temperatures as low as –60°C (–76°F).
- As many as 5 million Adélie penguins crowd together to lay eggs.
- Penguin parents that have lost their eggs might adopt other eggs—sometimes bits of broken shell—to care for.

Where in the World

A lone Magellanic penguin checks out a rugged island close to Argentina.

SEA-GOING BIRDS. That's what penguins are. Some kinds spend many months of each year at sea, only heading for land during breeding seasons.

Unlike other penguins, emperor penguins don't ever step foot on land. When they leave the water, they move onto the vast sheets of ice that form when the surface of the sea freezes over. Then they head back to the water to feed.

At the end of every year's breeding season, penguins molt, losing their old feathers and growing new ones. During those one to two weeks, the penguins can't enter the sea at all.

5

On the Galapagos Islands, a pair of Galapagos penguins climb a rocky shore.

Without their usually dense coats, the water would wet their skin, overcooling the penguins—even causing them to become sick and die.

Penguins are found only in the southern half of the world. Several kinds, such as the emperor and Adélie penguins, make their homes around Antarctica. Peruvian and Magellanic penguins live off South America. A number of kinds of penguins swim along the coasts and islands of Australia and New Zealand. And jackass penguins live near the tip of South Africa.

The penguins that have settled the farthest north—right near the equator—are named after their home. These Galapagos penguins settle among the Galapagos Islands, far from the coast of Ecuador, where a cold ocean current from Antarctica cools the water.

STAYING WARM, KEEPING COOL

Snow doesn't melt on penguins. Thick layers of fat and dense feather coats help keep body heat in—and cold air out. And special blood vessels prevent the penguins' feet from freezing without letting too much heat escape.

If penguins become overly hot, they cool off by panting, ruffling their feathers, and shaking their flippers. Penguins that live in warm climates also lose heat through patches of bare skin around their eyes and on their feet.

7

Water World

NO WONDER PENGUINS FEEL AT HOME IN THE WATER. Their bodies are built for swimming and diving. Unlike most other birds, penguins have solid—not hollow—bones that make them heavier and easier to submerge. Their flippers are strong and flat, like paddles. And their smooth feather coats allow the birds to slip easily through the water. Oil from glands beneath their tails waterproofs the feathers.

Of all birds, penguins are the best swimmers. They fly underwater by using their flippers for power and their webbed feet to steer. Some kinds can change

A penguin uses its super swimming skills to catch fish.

Flying underwater, a penguin frequently bursts from the sea to breathe.

direction suddenly by turning cartwheels.

Most penguins swim up to 10 kilometres (6 miles) per hour, but in bursts they might move twice that fast. Gentoo penguins are among the quickest swimmers, occasionally reaching 27 kilometres (17 miles) per hour.

As Adélie penguins leave the water, they often pick up enough speed to shoot right up in the air before landing on their feet. Erect-crested penguins sometimes ride swift waves to shore, then latch onto rocks, so they won't be carried back out to sea.

Penguins are amazing divers. Some kinds make shallow dives and can stay underwater for over two minutes. Other kinds dive much deeper. Emperor penguins can reach depths of 500 metres (1640 feet), holding their breath for about 20 minutes. Deep diving makes it possible for them to catch food such as squid.

CATCHING A BREATH OF AIR

As swimming penguins speed through the ocean, they never stop to breathe. Instead, they "porpoise" every few minutes. Surging out of the water with their flippers flapping, they snatch a few quick breaths of air, then plunge right back into the sea.

Leaping in and out of the ocean also serves another purpose. It creates little air bubbles that help the penguins glide more easily—and more swiftly—through the water.

World Full of Food

Sharp beaks and bristly tongues help penguins hold onto slimy food.

PENGUINS ALWAYS DINE AT SEA. They gobble up lots of fish and masses of tiny, shrimplike animals called krill. King and emperor penguins eat a lot of squid, which thrive in the cold waters off Antarctica.

When penguins chase down their dinners, they streamline their sleek bodies as much as possible. They pull their heads down close to their shoulders and hold their feet tightly against their bodies. Then the birds charge through the water, darting this way and that as they nab their prey. Penguins are as nimble as they are quick.

Seafood is slippery, so it's a good thing

13

penguins have beaks built for grabbing and holding. And their spiny tongues provide extra grip. Penguins flip the fish they catch, then swallow the prey headfirst and whole.

When penguins have young chicks to feed, they hunt for extra prey. Emperor penguins might each stuff themselves with

An emperor penguin feeds its chick a soupy meal of fish.

an additional 3 kilograms (7 pounds) of food to take to their newly hatched chicks. Back home, they bring up the partly digested meals, and the chicks feed by poking their tiny beaks into their parents' gaping ones.

If emperor chicks hatch before their mothers arrive with food to feed them, the father penguins give them "penguin milk." It's not real milk but a mixture of fat and protein. The meal oozes from a tube joining the penguin's throat with his stomach.

Scientists can tell which penguins have been eating plenty of fish and which penguins have been eating mostly krill. The proof is in the color of the waste, or guano (GWA-no), that the birds produce.

Fish-feeders tend to leave behind plenty of white guano, while krill-feeders excrete pink guano. What's more, some penguins, such as gentoos, can eat so much krill that the yolks of their eggs turn a deep pink—even red.

World of Words

"YAP, GRUNT, YAP, YAP," little penguins call to one another. Jackass penguins b-r-a-y like the donkeys they were named after. And around the antarctic, chinstrap penguins chatter loudly.

What's all the noise about? When it's time to breed, most kinds of penguins gather in large crowds. The males—the first to arrive at mating places, called rookeries—often HONK to claim their breeding or nesting spots.

Male Adélie penguins usually look for nests they have used in other years. When they find the nests, they wave their flippers

King penguins throng together, trying to attract and call mates.

17

around and holler, "Gug-gug-gug-gug-gaaaaa." That's how they announce, "This is mine!"

When female penguins arrive at a rookerie, the males call out to them. Standing tall, the male penguins toss back their heads and belt out "songs." Pairs that have mated before frequently find

With beaks open and pointed skyward, chin-strap penguins signal their interest in mating.

each other and become mates again. Other penguins attract new mates.

Two Adélie mates might stand face to face, rocking their heads forward and back. Then they point their beaks to the sky and cry out. It's their way of saying, "We're together. We're a pair."

Sometimes, penguin "talk" is used to sound alarms. If an Adélie penguin spots danger, such as a hungry leopard seal lurking in the water, it might make a noise that warns others, "Watch out!"

CRIES IN THE WIND

Winds howl fiercely across the islands where king penguins breed. The noise can make it hard for them to hear and find their mates.

King penguins can't change the pitch of their cries, and they can't holler louder. Instead, on windy days, they call more often, and they make more sounds in each call—12 in place of the usual 4. Frequent cries from both males and females have a better chance of being heard during dips in the wind's noise level.

World of Eggs

EGGS IN CAVES, EGGS IN BURROWS. Different kinds of penguins choose different places to lay their eggs. Many penguins prefer to lay the eggs right out in the open. The birds may fight with others to claim their laying spots, then guard them fiercely.

Some penguins build nests for their eggs. They use whatever material they can find—stones, grass, leaves, or twigs. Royal penguins have even made nests out of bones taken from old penguin skeletons.

Other kinds of penguins build no nests at all. Emperor and king penguins, for instance, simply cradle their eggs on the

A rockhopper penguin protects two eggs in its nest of grass.

21

Reshuffling its position, a gentoo penguin prepares to settle on an egg.

tops of their feet. Unlike most penguins, which produce two eggs at a time, emperor and king penguins lay just one each. They tuck it—not in pouches—but under a thick blanket of belly skin. There it stays warm even in the coldest of weather. An emperor or king penguin egg can take about two months to hatch.

Penguin mates work together to look after their eggs. Many males take the first shift, caring for the eggs while the females head back to sea to feed. When the females return to mind the eggs, the males eat.

While parent penguins are busy tending eggs and protecting them from other sea birds, they survive on nothing but their own body fat. During that time, the penguins can lose more than a third of their total weight.

EGGS ON THE ROCKS

In the windswept antarctic, Adélie penguins often nest at the base of rocky slopes or ice cliffs. Resting on their bellies, they scrape out the ground with sharp claws on their feet, then create small "bowls" by piling up pebbles. They try to make sure their nests are deep enough to stay dry. Flooding would cool the eggs laid inside.

If Adélie penguins have trouble finding pebbles for their own nests, they may steal some from others.

New World

PECK, PECK, PECK. Penguin chicks can take three days to break through the shell of their eggs. Then the parent birds warm and protect the chicks—as they cared for the eggs. Other sea birds—gulls, skuas, and giant petrels—can easily snatch unguarded chicks.

Along antarctic coasts, bold sea birds called sheathbills might steal food from penguin chicks. Just as a chinstrap penguin brings up a bit of half-digested krill to feed its chick, a sheathbill can dart between them, scooping up the meal.

As penguin chicks grow, some kinds

Fluffy and gray, an emperor chick looks nothing like adult emperor penguins.

Adélie penguins prepare to take rides on floating ice.

gather in groups for safety while their parents hunt for food. And by the time the chicks have thick, waterproof coats, most are ready to head off on their own. Many kinds of penguins leave when they're only two months old; others, when they're over a year.

Young penguins don't have to learn how to swim or hunt. They simply plunge into the water and do what comes naturally. They may discover a few enemies in the sea, such as fur seals and killer whales. Around antarctic ice slabs, called floes, leopard seals are the greatest threat. These fast swimmers skulk in the water, waiting to snap their powerful jaws at Adélie, gentoo, and rockhopper penguins.

Still, penguins that survive to adulthood will likely live several more years. Chinstrap and yellow-eyed penguins may reach age 15, at least.

GO WITH THE FLOE

Penguins don't spend much time at play. But some Adélie penguins seem to take rides for no reason other than just to have fun. Pushing and shoving, they line up to sail on the ice floes that drift by.

Leaping onto a passing floe, an Adélie penguin rides along for a short stretch before jumping back to shore. Then it may immediately rejoin the penguin line for a chance to take another ice floe ride.

Index